W9-BYM-426

Fighting for History

PATHFINDER EDITION

By Peter Winkler

CONTENTS

Across America, some people study th

Fighting

ivil War in a special way. They relive it.

History

By Peter Winkler

White smoke crept over a green field. The smoke teased people's eyes and noses. It seeped into their clothes.

Standing in the smoke were some 5,000 **reenactors.** Those are people who act out past events. They came to western Virginia to act out the Battle of Cedar Creek. It was a turning point of the Civil War. That struggle tore America apart during the 1860s.

For the reenactors, the 1864 battle was as real as the white smoke. "You actually get into the past," explained Lynn Peterson. Acting out the past, she said, is a great way to bring history to life. Across America, countless other people feel the same way.

The reenactors worked hard to get every detail right. Indeed, Cedar Creek looked as if time had stopped long ago. Tents stood in neat lines. Cooking pots simmered over campfires. Soldiers in blue and gray marched to the sound of drums.

A House Divided

It may be hard to imagine that Americans went to war against one another. But they did. How could this happen?

The answer lay in differences between the states. Northern states were fairly **industrial.** Many people worked in factories or shops.

The South was mainly **agricultural.** Most people worked on farms. They grew cotton, rice, sugarcane, tobacco, and other crops.

Raising those crops was hard work. To do it, some Southerners used African-American slaves. A slave was a person legally owned by another person. By 1860, nearly four million slaves worked in the United States.

Throughout the 1800s, Americans argued bitterly about slavery. Should they allow it in new states as the country grew? Could slavery continue in the South? Northerners and Southerners disagreed sharply about what to do. Somehow, though, Americans managed to stick together—barely.

☆ Disunited States ☆

Disagreements about slavery tore America apart during the 1860s. Union states (blue) remained loyal to the United States. Confederate states (gray) broke away to form a new country. Territories (tan) did not belong to any state at the time.

OREG.
MINN.
N.H.
ME.
VT.
WIS.
N.Y.
MASS.
MICH.
R.I.
IOWA
PA.
CONN.
U.S. TERRITORIES
ILL. IND.
OHIO
N.J.
W. VA.
DEL.
CALIF.
KANS.
MO.
KY.
VA.
MD.
TENN.
N.C.
ARK.
S.C.
MISS. ALA.
GA.
TEX.
LA.
FLA.

UNION STATES
CONFEDERATE STATES
TERRITORIES

N W E S

True Blue. *The North had many more factories than the South. So Union soldiers were better equipped than Confederates.*

The Blue and the Gray

Shades of Gray. *Gray was the South's official color. But many soldiers wore blue clothes taken from dead Northerners.*

An Uncivil War

The country broke apart in 1860. Abraham Lincoln was elected President. He opposed the spread of slavery. Many Southern leaders feared he would destroy their way of life.

South Carolina chose to **secede** from the United States in December 1860. Other states soon followed. They formed the Confederate States of America. Its people and soldiers were known as Confederates.

President Lincoln refused to let the Union, or country, split up. He said he would even use force to keep the South from seceding. In response, Confederates attacked Fort Sumter in South Carolina. War began.

From 1861 to 1865, the North and South fought fiercely. Three million soldiers served in the war. Keeping them fed was a big job.

Confederate troops got much of their food from the Shenandoah Valley. That's a region in Virginia. The South held the area for most of the war. Then came the summer of 1864.

Small Battle, Big Impact

That summer, Union troops marched into the valley. They wanted to cut the Confederates' food supply. That would really make it harder for the South to keep fighting.

On October 19, the two armies clashed at Cedar Creek. The Confederates nearly won. But the northern general urged his men to hang on. They did. The Union won the battle.

Cedar Creek affected the war in two big ways. The Union gained control over the Shenandoah Valley. The victory also cheered the weary North. In fact, the news probably helped Lincoln get reelected a few weeks later.

The war lasted just months after Cedar Creek. In April 1865, both sides met in a Virginia town. The South surrendered. Union soldiers began cheering, but their leader stopped them. "The war is over," he said. "The **rebels** are our countrymen again."

Getting It Right

October 2004 was the 140th anniversary of the Battle of Cedar Creek. Reenactors were excited to relive this event. As always, they tried to do it just right. Brian Barron knows that.

Brian, you see, acted as a Confederate drummer. He also plays in the school band. But Civil War drummers held their sticks differently. It's a small detail, but that's part of living history. So Brian learned to play his drum the old-fashioned way.

Megan Wright worked hard on details too. She learned the Virginia reel, waltz, and other 19th-century dances. And her old-style skirt reached the ground. Hoops pushed the fabric into a wide circle. "I love these outfits," she said. "I'd wear them to school if I could."

The Power of the Past

Young or old, the reenactors marveled at the power of their shared effort. Grown men talked about the terror of facing line after line of enemy soldiers.

Some moments cut too deep for words, said Lew Ulrich. "You think about folks dying on this same ground," he continued. "One guy sat in his tent crying. That's how much it affects you." History can do that.

If you were a Civil War reenactor, would you fight for the North or for the South? Why?

★ Wordwise ★

agricultural: based on farming

industrial: based on making and selling things

rebel: person fighting against his or her own country

reenactor: one who acts out the past

secede: break away

Drummer Boy. *"It's fun to be out here,"* said Confederate reenactor Max Glazier. Thousands of boys served as Civil War drummers. Drumbeats helped soldiers march properly.

AMARIA STENZEL (USS CONSTITUTION); BATES LITTLEHALES (COINS).

History

On the battleground at Cedar Creek, people got together to act out an important event. The experience helped them better understand the Civil War. But you don't have to be a reenactor to see history in action. It's as easy as going to a historical park.

There are more than a hundred historical parks and monuments in the United States. Each of these sites lets you step back in time. You can sense what our country was like at different times and in different places.

Let's explore four sites that celebrate people and events of the past. Take a close look at each. How do these parks and monuments bring history to life?

Boston National Historical Park

The Boston National Historical Park is a series of sites in Boston, Massachusetts. You don't need a guide or a map to explore this park. Just take the Freedom Trail. This is a red line painted on the sidewalk. Follow the line as it winds around town. Each stop on the Freedom Trail gives you a unique view of our country's independence.

At some sites, you will find people dressed in period clothing. They pretend to be living during the American Revolution. You can even meet people planning the Boston Tea Party! You might also step on board the U.S.S. *Constitution.* Learn how this famous ship got its nickname, "Old Ironsides."

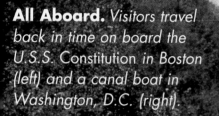

All Aboard. *Visitors travel back in time on board the U.S.S.* Constitution *in Boston (left) and a canal boat in Washington, D.C. (right).*

rought to Life

The C&O Canal

The Chesapeake & Ohio Canal National Historical Park offers a different view of American life. This park runs along the C&O Canal. The canal is more than 184 miles long. It runs from Washington, D.C., all the way to Cumberland, Maryland. Each section of the canal was built by hand.

The canal was like a road made of water. Between 1828 and 1924, people used it for shipping. Boats carried coal and other goods, such as building supplies and food.

Moving goods on the canal wasn't easy, though. Canal boats didn't have motors. How did these heavy boats move from place to place? Mules pulled them!

On the Water

A dirt trail called a towpath runs beside the canal. Mules walked along the towpath. They pulled the canal boats with ropes. That's how boats traveled along the waterway.

The C&O Canal was a shipping center for more than a century. Today, canal boats no longer carry goods. Now they carry visitors.

In Washington, D.C., you can catch a ride on a real canal boat. Listen as the guide tells stories. You'll learn about the people who lived and worked on the canal. You'll find out why building the C&O Canal was so hard. You'll even learn how railroads put the canal out of business. As you move down the canal, you'll feel like you're traveling back in time.

Climbing Into the Past.
Visitors can explore ancient cliffside homes at Bandelier National Monument.

Bandelier National Monument

The Bandelier National Monument is a place where you can explore both nature and history. Bandelier is located in the steep cliffs and deep canyons of New Mexico. The Jemez Mountains are to the west of the park. The Rio Grande River flows east of the park.

At Bandelier, you can explore waterfalls and trails. You can also discover Native American history. Hundreds of ancient Pueblo homes are tucked in the canyons. Some are in caves or along canyon walls. Others are part of stone cities at the tops of the steep cliffs. The Pueblo lived in the area of Bandelier more than a thousand years ago. Their homes let visitors explore ancient ways of life.

Exploring the Past

To step back in time at Bandelier, pull on a good pair of hiking boots. Begin your journey by hiking along the Main Loop Trail. It winds past some excavated, or uncovered, Pueblo homes. Along the way, climb up wooden ladders into ancient cliffside homes. Explore the rooms where the Pueblo cooked and slept centuries ago.

After your hike, be sure to check out the special events at Bandelier. For example, you can make crafts with local Native Americans. When the sun goes down, you can also join a ranger for a night walk. This is a silent walk in the darkness through some of the park's most interesting sites.

A Dark History. *At the Alcatraz prison, people tour cells that once held dangerous criminals.*

Alcatraz Island

Historical parks can also give you a view of America's more recent past. That's the case at Alcatraz Island. Alcatraz is off the coast of California. From the 1930s to the 1960s, this island housed a prison. Some of the country's worst criminals were held as prisoners here.

Today, you can explore the prison. To get there, ride a boat from San Francisco. When you arrive, head to a theater near the dock. There you can watch a short movie about the island and its famous prison. After the show, stroll up to the prison. Take a tour with a park ranger to find out what it was like to live and work within the prison walls.

More History to Explore

There are many ways to learn about history. You can read a book, watch a film, or go online. But if you want to see, hear, and smell details of the past, you may want to head for a historical site.

From coast to coast, these monuments and parks give visitors special views into the past. They let people discover history in even the most unexpected places.

You can sail in ships and ride canal boats. You can climb through ancient homes. You can meet people who talk and dress like Americans who lived long ago. At historical parks and monuments, you don't just read about the past. You experience it firsthand.

Living History

Take a shot at these questions to find out what you learned from the book.

1 Why did southern states want to secede from the country?

2 Why was the Battle of Cedar Creek important?

3 What are reenactors? Why do you think they pay attention to small details?

4 How is visiting a historical park different from reading about history in a book?

5 Which historical park would you most like to visit? Why?

★ ★ ★ ★